Sea GATE

JOCELYN EMERSON

Alice James Books
Farmington, Maine

10 9 8 7 6 5 4 3 2 1

Alice James Books are published by Alice James Poetry Cooperative, Inc.,
an affiliate of the University of Maine at Farmington.

Alice James Books
238 Main Street
Farmington, ME 04938
www.umf.maine.edu / ~ajb

Library of Congress Cataloging-in-Publication Data
Emerson, Jocelyn
Sea gate / Jocelyn Emerson.
p. cm.
ISBN 1-882295-35-8
1. Title.
PS3605.M48 S43 2002
811'.6—dc21
2002004570

Alice James Book gratefully acknowledges support from the University
of Maine at Farmington and the National Endowment for the Arts.

Cover image: Gabor Petardi, *Land, Sea and Moon.* 1967.262.
Smithsonian American Art Museum.

CONTENTS

ACKNOWLEDGMENTS

Grateful acknowledgment is made to the editors and staff of the following publications in which these poems first appeared, sometimes in earlier versions:

American Letters & Commentary: from "Sea Gate" section V as "Moving Stones"; *American Literary Review:* "Where Breath Most Breathes"; *Barrow Street:* "The Veil" (p. 42); *Black Warrior Review (Warrior Web):* "On the Apparition of a Substantive," "Black Veil"; *Colorado Review:* "Iteration (I)" as "Bridge," "The Lighthouse," "Iteration (II)" as "Bridge," "Equinox"; *Cutbank:* "Of Doubt and Lineament," from "Sea Gate" section IX as "Zero"; *Denver Quarterly:* "Ere Long," "Apophatic"; *Epoch:* "Palinode," "Via Negativa"; *Iowa Journal of Cultural Studies:* "The Veil" (p. 35); *New American Writing:* from "Sea Gate" section III as "Iteration III," section VII as "Iteration VI," "The Conflagration"; *Poet Lore:* "Rain" as "Equinox," "The Rivers We're Eyeing"; *Seneca Review:* "Night Blindness"; *Sojourner:* "As Slightly as the Routes of Stars" as "Hallowmas."

A different version of "Sea Gate" originally appeared as a chapbook, *Confirmations of the Rapt* (Red Dog Press) designed by Judy Jensen.

My deepest gratitude to Jim Emerson, Reginald Shepherd, Mark Slawson, Lara Trubowitz and Geffin Falken; their sustaining support brought this book into being. Love and thanks to my parents, Joy and Robert Emerson. It is a privilege to express my appreciation to all of my teachers and to acknowledge my abiding gratitude to Cheryl McNeily. Love and thanks to Jayson Barsic, Tammy Emerson, Nancy Granert, Valerie Long, Chris Merrill, Amy Peterson, Tania Pryputniewicz, Patricia Reid, Kelly Ritter, Deb West and Arline Wyler. And to S.V., for her heart.

. . . wind for the kite and kite for the wind,
even when the sky is missing.

—Odysseas Elytis
"Annoint the Ariston" (X)

To Olga Broumas

and in memory of
Brett Hobbie
(1965 – 1992)

NIGHT BLINDNESS

Beneath any common belief
lies the unspoken, occluded, torn
way we proceed. (On the beach
we were washed clean by transverse
waves.) All day long, on these
two lanes, gulls let clams and other
mollusks drop from their beaks—
the animals, raw, inside—
(at first, black sinew held fast
the hinge on each shattered,
calcareous shell). Then we
were driving between dunes
(riding time) on a glacial carved
landscape—out to Race Point—
much as a word travels through
the sensorial inner ear to the cranial
space. Now satellites transmit
the originating explosion, traced
in the fossil radiation, an echo
of singularity carried on rip-tides
of electromagnetic waves—
carrying forth the broken symmetry—
And no rain in weeks.
A chalky road illuminates
a place.

I

Save that my soul's imaginary sight
Presents thy shadow to my sightless view...

— *Shakespeare's Sonnets, 27*

ERE LONG

Who would awaken from the bright means—

      from an idleness inside the havoc of August
into the slack gutturals of autumn harnessing
      everything at its vanishing point—
and be seen catching each fluctuation at the moment
we want to inhabit it

      only to inherit the vacancy at the center of a promise?
What watermark, what chime or thistle might draw out
this pain, binding me to . . . .
      Barley water, and sheaves, are things I'd bring her
(as she awakened among birds with hidden wings)
      and would I find, in the measure of those pinioned
wings, the whole form of desire?

      Statue, feather, summons *(stain the ground red*
with ocher to stimulate a fast rebirth—)
      And woods are in the asking: I ate from the timbrel,
I drank from the cymbal, I carried the kernos,
      I passed beneath the pastos.
Petitions, celebrants, initiates, *Eleusias*—

§

      And then I walked after the summer's surge
along the spillway, along the channel dug,
along the possible horizontal sea floor, in the luxury
      of long, exposed fractures. I watched people getting them
on film with hand held cameras—concentrating on
      the stresses in the brittle sedimentary strata—

seeing in the once soft limestone the abundant
and the preserved *(hexagenaria, crinoids)* that accumulation
(calcium carbonate) in one afternoon,

in an hour *(irregular compaction)* loosed

and flooded with what the corrupted structure reveals:
the vanishing point of soil, in a few minutes,
(atonal stutter) and fossils, here in their double continuation
(formed) (seen), in the washing away
that's become the visible temperate.

§

After the water, I heard her atoms in me,
diffuse, in my body. I thought of this (at the time) as belief—
the molecules stilling in me, as fast as the inaudible—
a trace of her voice.

And I would that she reached us, each of us, this way, after,
making me entire in my waiting
as I was taken, in that moment, by her progress through

the interrupted promise—

where she begins again in me
at my vanishing point, in my idleness

by the river, near its justice, its ashen means—

A VEIL OF MULTIPLE ORDERS

shined as the first detail.
>   All forms prolong its shape—
the sea, as if etched to the page—

>   An undertow of wind curtails
sharp distinctions, stirring among them,
>   making former erasures brilliant
>   again . . . .

Drifting between nothing
>   and sign,
the veil rustled amid April's rapid certainties,
>   lifting in the remove between form
and form

(a stilled vowel quickening
at the center of a consonant-shift)

>   like the dark hammered-gold dust rising
out of summer's future stratagems
>   (startled in the wind's spatial memory,
>   towels, fluttering, at the rails)

as the sea's blunting hue settles amid
>   these rocks, the waves' slanting precision
holding them true.

ITERATION (I)

A light flickered. No more than
    that chorus, that minute
attenuation of the scene and a bough
    is falling, breaking the ashen water
a river there below to suck in all
    the air-notes and with them,
a visible world turning inward.
    A bough, just there,
and then caught up before one can ask
    let it be done so
(but not before one guesses for whom
    this gesture of being saved
was intended). Any possibility that desire
    and intention were wed just
now? Painted and spoken of: a river
    is being asked to fulfill *what*?
And I have scattered some seed to migrant
    birds, their wings dirty and light
alike, vocalizing what progress they have
    made toward the blossomed air of another
climate (time as dilated and expanded by weather)
    whether or not one speaks of birds
or of how those words would sound
    spoken from that far
shore where the bough will exclude itself
    from both this *drift* (called water)
and from *inhabitation* (here called bridge)
    in the traversable world—the edging
afternoon already far on its way to hollowing
    the well-rehearsed human voice—

AS SLIGHTLY AS THE ROUTES OF STARS

oak leaves fell on the lake
as part of the rain's work.
I stood on the porch watching
a blue-gray heron in flight
(its minute across the water).
A week before she died,
I dreamed we were rowing.
She pulled with an oar of light
wood. I was behind her,
with an oar of stone, turbulent
waves in a voice of every thing
made singular again, returning
to pure particle. No *letting go*,
only this difference, spreading—
matter breaking and becoming
light, fluent—this paradox of
irreconcilable grief and her new,
profuse listening: two rowers
on the same side of a boat
miraculously moving forward.

OF DOUBT AND LINEAMENT

A sudden rain pursues its wreckage.

> All along, water stored up in the wind's labor
finds duration there
>> (rain fast along the metalloid night)
>> (rain slow along the architectural day)
>>> each giving way to the other
within the impervious air.

> And then an invention between them *gleams*—
a repose between them summoning its own expression—
>> all rough transcription of the spirit.

§

>> And where light had settled.
>> And where dark is settling.

§

Leaves collect in the yard's north corner, gathering up
at the sagging fence (a few blowing back across: twos, threes).

Then rain distributes its way again along the houses—
along the barn—
>> glinting at the point of absorption.

§

Hours later,
frost attests to the rain's concealment
          (to one abstraction and its subsequent designs).
For now, all designs.

§

Circling crows, cut the arc and descend.
          Quick *drifts* and again the cut—
a resting on the pattern—
          on the occasional resolute updraft

of blue-black birds lighting a jagged current
          they're making between two newly outlined
elms.

II

THE LIGHTHOUSE

i.

Impatient with spring's incendiary budding, we longed for the irreconcilable tossing of summer's phenomenal vowels: brief cawing from gulls on the pilings to divide and overturn May's minor successes (that profusion of greens rubbing against the loosened pane). We watched as an afternoon was laid over the afternoons, like rain on the sea. Renting one of the many clattering skiffs in which to reach the peninsula, we traversed an idea of space and saturation all the way out to where the phosphorous shards of early evening grew hard with a deepening friction. Occasionally the lacunae between stars would glow dimly—stars which became, under different names each night, our ardent relief—a cool and continuous wake left by scores of April violets.

ii.

More than a pyrrhic discovery—clusters of Queen Anne's lace through which the wind inscribes a muted text. Salt air burns the last of winter's damp cordwood to ash. The weathervane spins inside a set of parallel winds. By our road, the heavy monody of goldenrod. The first June lily opened its whitest furl—the field itself in an hour of heliotropic origin. After that, we liked the way the tight equation of waves went on finishing nothing among the many drifts of seaweed swaying all day at the fray.

iii.

Of the types of inflorescence, she liked compound umbel and
corymb best—wild carrot and cherry—variation of structuring
root, pith and stem. What became of the leaky skiff, its aluminum
tuned to thinness by this water's relentless logarithm? The days
themselves became fractions of polished metal, tuneless numbers,
as the acute and accurate boat was worn away by reference, and by
our other forms of luminous inquiry. The bay dispersed the heat
of our instincts until the boat became the question of a trans-
parency gained through travel. So long exposed to those elemen-
tal particulars, the boat is hard to conceive of—moving as it does
between one ideal shore and another—just an inference of relation
with seldom a trace to be spoken of. Then, just an open sea to
hold the boat's oscillations, the echoes of its cold-burning song.

iv.

It was the effort of sifting through August's scattered abeyance
which awakened our love of autumn's delay—that voice of its
tonal gesture in a phonemic drift through which vowels were only
so many moorings—boats in the harbor. Every so often the gulls'
pitch reduced the day's amplitude to fractions of its blue equation,
leaving the wooden piles of consonants with which our nights
were built. Not the view, but the window glass (long past molten)
was our perspective on this sea's refracting tones. Outside, a
wind's thin tremolo through dunes would light or delay our sleep.
We knew how suddenly the idea of a more distant paradise leaves
you.

III

This fabulous shadow only the sea keeps.

— Hart Crane

SEA GATE

I

Encumbered water, salt drift and reticent
silver-green of this desiring form:

diurnal, approximant, virtual and enflamed—
hurled and hallowed in brief mimicry—

In our momentum, the sylvan errand,
and wave function.

Such variance ensconced in salt,
a capella the broken laughter.

Strange to choose all pause and impetus
slower by turns, *brain, sinew, bone*:

all periodicity and diffraction to a body go . . .
Odd symmetry to fasten the phenomena

and enumerate the root and drought,
O errant garment—

ambient form and bounded atmosphere—
Here is isometric display, all limb and agape,

(enumerate, around, minimum, implicate)
All naught. The specter and the scripting.

To postulate a fissure in the wind's engine.
All course. *No, boundlessness.*

II

Understand the troubling lexicon
of an intractable body,

its measured interdiction
joined to odds of sight

in this fluorescent verisimilitude
without mirror across the water

and crossing the water before me.
A particular skill to become the symmetry

of radium and wing (and not intervene)
learning the new motions of a multiple

and parabolic construction, the wild
hypotheses of the inner ear, the illness

and equilibrium of unseasonable whiteness—
that unseen provenance I cannot still—

III

Disembark. Drag and shift in sacrifice.
Entreat.

Resume stature and aspect:
subaltern terror seized.

Dint of this investiture
in copper, and sea rain

(anaphoric statuary, tensile speech)
(rigid with refuse and the dust of stars)

In early morning, the haul of cod piled.
An intrinsic and featureless thing.

Prolific sun on the field of quick,
the field of implement.

Carriage and carcass of nonchalance.
Stark muscle.

Traversing vessel, in reprieve.
Vanquished hull, moored in port.

I will remember you.
Another song too.

Blood washed from it.

IV

Let us turn then, open-mouthed,
from dimension to dimension

without sorrow like hungry wind
working leaves to contingency.

(Show me what abstinence spares—
what radiance is its furthest version

of aftermath without a listing sky—
what denial mends the grieving eye?)

Make of it some geometric form, some
hummingbird, some bleating word.

V

Herds of the day
called home.
Was a face you knew.
Across moved
this migration—
perfected body gazing back—
skin of weather taut
along high zeros
of a nervous system
performing in isolation.
We call the herds,
colored with migration,
home. To trade for them
a weather of skin.
(This becomes the tendency
of weather to cross a sky.)
We did not know.
To color it risen,
like a nervous system
inscribing the sky's
perfect body, children
at play in the game
of hidden herds, naming
tribes of systems
across a day. Sky
in zero migration.

VI

Then a blizzard covers
in wider motion.

A public presence
although materially

nothing is its one cold puzzle—
its fibrous, insomniac valence—

A voice asking to stay longer,
to excavate a vivid subject

from the syllables of this newly
whitening idiom

antecedents becoming some beautiful
secondary lining of the plenum.

Suddenly the irremissible, like snow . . .
and the seemingly inert intervals.

Then there's roadside cowslip
and the white and red blossoming apple—

all the confirmations of the rapt—
And intimacies, like driven sand.

VII

"Volumes now
where a substitute

was avidly
displayed

in such steady
remove—

always
cautionary—

A proposition
you'd made.

Laws were probabilities
were decimals.

It was an other
more often resembled,

attentive with lack
and distraction.

Late dawn, I thought
entropy resolved

the sensational logic
of a consuming absence

on the edge of
speaking itself—

rocky sustenance.
Comparisons help

with what is irreversible."
Anchor as anchor.

VIII

Nobody's in the wake of the heavy
swells, the grainy black rains

(ignorant of brilliant sky
and constructing plateaus

and repetitions of self, poured
and floating toward chordal stir)

All increase, for example.
All extinguishing example.

With sun, repetition no longer occupies
a flaying light—

Now an instantaneous musculature,
and an exodus of dust in ordinary ends—

We paint the iron tables a parallel blue.
We count them as facts.

IX

In a remnant language,
with false specificity,

we spoke of certain helices
as clean codes of history

(rust in the wind, half-cities
burning in the night)

and of the displacement
between position and momentum

as a new existence beginning
in all the improbable anatomies—

commercial, empirical—
in the ruins of the will.

X

Cloud's edge. Imperceptible, scant fissure. A few
    admonitions.
Stochastic plane spelled in the sheltering relationship
    of flesh
and blood. Battered pier. Columns bleached. And
    wind's
just now setting out a boundary composed of iteration
    with all
the littering motion of errors—not in relationship to any
    city nor lit
by an altering image—. Follow like actual water, into silt
    and toil.

XI

Into the prerogative stir
       of the remove, of the strange hour
of the nothing more.

       Pure sublunary
annulled September, angle and frost
its burnt offering.

Peculiar solace
       to wander without occasion
in this obedient and obdurate

mourning—not for punishment,
       nor the insatiable trades
of antinomy thus conferred—

IV

And thought . . . is at the limit of this conflagration,
like a candle blown out at the limit of a flame.

—Georges Bataille

ON THE APPARITION
OF A SUBSTANTIVE

I.

Between both moons . . .
listening to waves shaped
by the wind's weights,
to an intonable solitude
in the human voice—
its interior denudation—

Before dying and after living . . .
the wind's lines draw me
down and hold me still
to be crossed—
then inscribed by the rising
element—

II.

We are a bone of looking
lying beside a sea . . .
through a bright
isotropic recess, returning
clouds cast us along the sea—
prefigured in the stilled narrative—

reaching toward an *a priori* sky, a divided sky, an anvil sky

(broken words from whole relics)

III.

And quickly dissipating
through living wind,
and enough weather.
Concordant fragrance.

Simple, aromatic
confluence.

That never begins . . . .

IV.

Impossible to say what happens there—
in the missing mass—

Only a sea, barely visible.
Ions. And wind.
Then, that prepossessing
cartilage of waves
breaking over the shores
of human delight . . . .

THE VEIL

And all too soon, one must look to the surface—

and among surfaces—for a continuum residing in layers.
        Recesses of color coalesce on the canvas:
all former matter of details leaking through
                                until I see configuration
(residual) pressing forward between the few
vertical lines—

        Transparent or dense, I think the idyllic pools
at the peripheries of the veil—itself the very form of *tending*
        toward (here the blue arriving at weightiness,
the red at delayed fluidity).

        Assuming the white border
somewhere in my sight (keep it visible, the fabric stretched, mobile)
        I see, meanwhile, that color
has been spreading all this time (as intended)
        to its possible edges—

ITERATION (II)

Still, the wind is in the middle of *telling*
          something to the river which is in the middle
of *describing* it . . . their indefinite discourse
          fanned in quick, mute patches—
exposed fractions of the light's interior—
          Then I hear the form
this lucid green bank is making along both
          sides of the *version* now transcribing
itself between them—fragments of it here
          in these places of slightly upturned
surface—
                 On the bridge, traffic settles
into its slow possession of the day—
          just after the height of its attachment
rush hour—And beneath, this approach going on,
          sunk deep in its one consequence,
down into which I'm looking at a few shadows
          there (inside the dark of the situation)
down into this long slippage as a purpose
          given into (but something's purified
as it flies back up the river's stair, back up through
          the motion it hears inside the shadow).
                    I look down
at the spectral memory, at the precision
          of its repeated liquidity,
down into the course of it as it verifies

its own origin—then at a few
circles on the water's dimension—
    until they're taken back up
into the means in which they once held
    their form: watching as they're carried
until something like a wave
    begins.

THE RIVERS WE'RE EYEING

In what body will I lie down?

          Smoke rises from the field's darkened rim.
Shall it lead me though these palpable moods
          (the day's cerulean permutations)
(the afternoon's irresolution)
          and into the curvature of time?

                    A cold, constant rain traces
the intricate vacancies of a river's fallow
          route. Then, in the dried basin, weeds glitter
with all the new contingencies

          (waters we carried on our backs, waters now
too infected to drink from, the waters of our anguishing labor
          and the waters after, of our freeing labor . . .).

In the incremental gusts of winter's duration beginning,
in several sequential darknesses, beginning,

what necessary indeterminacy transfigures
          both this dry swale and the river now running some miles
behind us—

          its sometimes shallows, its sometimes depths—

EQUINOX

Or so it seems, lately. How preoccupied I am with spurious
ideas regarding the wild circumference of influence—
looking as I did to the jimsonweed
at midsummer for proof that the scrape and catch
of mourning's narrative details can thicken,
again, the flood-eroded field—dispersing
over its surface of bare brown arrival, signs
(identical to one another) of the first acts
of disclosure—thinking my own haste will work
like the weeds' and displace the weight
of light's *a priori*, featureless, space.
But the equinox is a summer's consequence:
day and night sharing an intersected ecliptic
(as alike as they are not alike)
the diaphanous line (a thread of voice)
connecting them; they grow no closer.
I look again at a picture I love, taken
one early spring, the haze of pink
(hydrangea petals?) drawing my gaze
deeper into the leaves, past the foreground
of white magnolias and her white blouse:
that white upon which seeing the other
colors depends.

ARCHITECTURE (II)

Assurances—the way in our absence, things repair themselves:
    the old barn leaning, birds nesting, allowing a common good
        to arrive sometime after. All along, a life
            of endless etceteras.

Can music be split open to reveal age, cosmologies—
    something about generations of families and the end
        of eras? Then one reaches to turn off the tape,
            getting up for a brief walk.

What then is the purpose of measuring this world through reason?
    At the finality (smooth ending of the quartet) only
        more particles—still *divisible*—then sadness,
            and no questions anymore.

And the tongue then burneth fiercely, and the parched throat is inflamed:
    the beauty of the eyes . . . . When is one no longer listening
        to a fleeting sound (to intervals of distance)
            or those distances between?

In longitudinal waves I've learned to hear a displacement
    increasing between the compression and the rarefaction:
        all through this darkness structured more fully than light,
            space and time beating level,

and corresponding only to the diamond in the eye.

OF A BARRED AND PALE LIGHT

October. The sea wind's standing chant
releases a wheeling year from its trials.

Leaves, blown in a commotion through
the morning's constellated sieves, absorb frost

as their bitter precursor, their reds and yellows
(long-waves and brief extremes of the visible spectrum)

revealing an equal splendor. How many times I've seen
waves locked in their rhythmic body, some nights

casting these weighted nets very far up; such a vowel,
kept constant over miles of coastline, subtracts detritus

from its shores: iodic seaweed, strewn rock and broken
shells dragging into cadence (scratches over the sound,

hum beneath). A half-moon nailed fast, water on sand
below, chanting an avowal, insistent on finishing . . . .

For all its quickening accretions, this month's an annulling
instant drawing the appreciable scattering into undertow—

clear days, resonating with an impersonal and intimate
future, becoming the shared artifice in which our separate,

intricate acts of speech are finished—wedding the waking
tongue to tattered utterance.

THE VEIL

is the most visible color
       of the intermediary, of alignment
(sheer gray-blue)

as the weather's destinationless drift accrues into the cold
            wind of December's inaudible garment

lying across the fast burning field—
lying down over summer's burnt facts—
            now all sequences in sequence itself:
shining, disparate residue over the firmament . . .

until the immobile becomes visible, again, in the place
       of its turning, in the system

(this crossing over of the veil)

such as when the whole glass we knew as summer
       shattered at the point of exact pitch,
       (releasing us from the *toward*)

such as light's exacting mercy,
       again through this whole corridor of winter
filling—

BLACK VEIL

1.

Only this morning a slight frost came over the panes,
and at mid-day the parchment of glass was there

      fixed and slow under natural digressions
of air and water,
          under a long, freezing pulse of wind
quickening and knotting (outside the sun's looking) on what
we call *the surface*—
         the glance (inside) fragmenting
against the glass—

across which weather is setting its designs.

2.

      Between wind's staves (it's 18°)
do you hear the shadow coming forth?
        (reigning in all the facts, all the true things)
Something like a disturbance and a destination
        begins to cross the day, glinting off
each thing at the place of its immunity

in the location of its nature (in the still motion of its design, mortal)

      The eye ceases
to measure (suddenly allied with time?)

                    how the light's pulse beats
        on each mechanism, in all of the organic clusters . . . .

But as the river is perfecting the minutes (one by one)—
        tossing between them, opening in them,
        the water's dithyrambs—

Afternoon's little *thrushes* —

                              3.

In this silver architecture of the day's confinement,
        the new steel building eyes the river's familiarity,
(ongoing in this, its minimizing strategy)

It's all reflection against the changes around it—
        degrees of gray, keeping time with the sky's cloudy
exchanges—
        something like sight, in the upper reaches of its light

        (no longer imprinted with former bright labors)
        (the river's erasure, the building's unoccupied structure)

A beating glance, through the shadow's whole distance, rushes—

V

ITERATION (III)

The bank's postponement lets
the river's mute rhetoric work
    the text of a day's heat
into a late, glinting occasion—
    shining city and quick daffodils—
this *being-seen* framed by the river's
    inexhaustible either/or . . .

a waiting arranged over
    and over by wind;
hearing its present tense fracturing
    in each direction
how can she listen into the water's passage,
    into the sourceless exposure
of its means? Or into the nonchalant
    suppletion of its end?
        She listens

for a trace of distinction
    all the way through
(the brassy ruptures of sun-down
    filling the windows . . .)
until the river's surface is weighted, again,
    with a night's fathomless
interest.

IMAGINARY WEATHER

1.

The year is late. The Northern Cross appears.
Six rivets of light, their attraction inversely proportional . . . .
 In Cassiopeia, Brahe's brilliant, sublunary
addition of 1572

2.

displaced belief in a single, objective point
 of observation—
impelling the eye—
 Through what accretion, or division,
are we reflected in a constellation's core?
 By what change in form
of movement are we altered, in our own mass?

3.

In the lower atmosphere, drifting stratus displays
a stratified enunciation—

 a long, displacing glance—

4.

The slight residue of rain taps on the roof:
 unexpected dissipation
glancing all the forms (footbridge, street lamp)
 wind picking up, holding each
in an imaginary singularity, carrying
 one leaf into brief postponement.

5.

Outside a half-lit mall, along the walkways,
bare ginkgoes threaded by the wrens' caterwaul—
        a patterned plenitude illuminating the facade
brick by brick—
                Buses pull out, mid-phrasing the night.

6.

In the midst of half-illumination,
        all transformability, beginning . . .

7.

in the austere watchfulness.

8.

With effort, with the minute by minute of mortal design
                (reflection, inflection, substance
for light's absorption)

9.

what spirit is again shaped by this formless wind,
                its invariant rest reconfigured and singing
in the form of physical song

        its particulate and finite flight?

SPRING ARGUMENT

So will the song carry into alteration

between midwinter's contending winds—
        until a kind of description is completed and torn
from human preoccupation—

                        (I heard it floating a little way along
February's thinning current of suggestion
            whose once early sway inhabited what it implied.)

                    So will the song then carry me within
the assailing passage it's made
            (like a wind deep inside another wind,
living without a May or a June to come)

            as it shifts, lightly, in the adventive fennel—
releasing the balm in the plant's manifold uses—

giving brief, aromatic bending to the bond.

THE VEIL

I.
Then, traces of hyphenated-dark rain
      on the white planks, making them whiter . . .

      given the rain's hold on an hour,
given the fortitude of summer's arrival
      swelling, with its green methodology,
the million-fold filament of spring's
articulation . . . .

Strands of stratified cloud drift and wane:
               wind forming as it is formed
by what it contains.

The wild columbine blows.

II.
Wrested from an hour's rigid gale,
the curve grows visible again in March,

       like the ash-burnished markings
       on winter's soundless seam.

I listen to a whole hour clustering
       its momentum, until the rhythm's sufficient to disperse
the month's concentrated breath—

       to be sorted again, through April's concerted speech—

How to keep a mediating netting of thought
       through entropy's flawless reach . . .
my voice adding nothing to this measure
       of wind already grown fuller through trees

winnowing its gale, in the other spring.

RAIN

It's insistent at the threshold.
Under the dowsing rod of a pale,
March sun, the wild attention of bitter
roadside nettles begins. Even the thin
timbre of private grief begins to endow
a habitat, its shifting form signified
in the whorled leaves of the cleaver weed.
These feathery greens of yarrow may be
an anodyne to break a seasonal fever.
(In time, her voice too was scraped
away on shoals of the disquieting day.)
The register of rain grows occasional,
its assurance enough to startle
a world composed of suggestion—
until all the whitened mouths
of the shepherds purse are open—
and the red clover has put down
its deep tap root. In a greening swath,
before the cutting, such rustling
disperses my anxious litanies—
the pollen from axillary buds filling
a lateral wind—and endowing
the light's approach with restoration's
instruments.

THE VEIL

is gone. The green is all transport.

A heavy white vase holds the arcs
and half-arcs of variegated, purple phlox . . .
                    (what subtle sheen the veil attains
in the night sky's isolate speech).

The listener listens among lessening
            repetitions of phrase which remind
(but are not manifest)

reinventing the green hour as a source of air—
            as some pale stirring at the center of the night's expanse—
voluminous ellipsis.

All along, was the veil itself that spectrum of green
grown thin, grown clear of resonance?

§

A listener becomes an iridescent core of description:
            particular sounds (*now* particle, *now* wave)
no longer form the delay
            signifying a word's fulfillment . . . .

The flow of surface—*earthly, equal, green in motion*—
            is that same happiness within which we loved the artifacts
of visible sight
            (vase of white phlox, and the radiant apples on the table)

in the original bright flux of each other's comfort, kind.

WHERE BREATH MOST BREATHES

I love and do not love these splendid
sea birds battered through various
days and slipping into discoloration
in the level darknesses of late March.
Under them, the drawn waves ending
as innate friction. Ore, and undulation.
(What rigging for traveling a voyaging
field?) The summer's excavation
takes the partial and the discrete,
struck out with loud report. A tidal inlet.
Lampblack and cold fluid together.
Listen to the scale of varied day,
shaken singer, to the charred song
of the particle and of the mineral ash,
still and elemental in the whistling dark.

VI

Darkness there was at first by darkness hidden . . .

Hymn of Creation, the *Rig-Veda*

THE CONFLAGRATION

I.
It was more just burning
than blowing together
to blaze—

punishment spoken from out
of a whirlwind—

We know this wound,
its stroke of pain,

in the oceanic dislocation
of subject . . . .

II.
In this morning's locution
of early spring,

a burning-cold and salt wave's
illegible contradiction

is splintering in tumult,
self-disclosed bright staves

spilling a sea-harvest
of insinuations.

In water, rich in nourishing
phosphates,

(deficient now in oxygen)
begins the invisible properties

of a body's lasting warmth . . . .

III.
(How a speech of breakers—
rock salt, crushed glass, poison ivy—

administered fire to the senseless
infection.)

IV.
And these knots of kelp keep and swell
the waves' peripheral, plural sway—

neither active nor passive, and refracting
almost all light—

save for the distance of event, save for
the distance of an extant sea's indifferent

obligation of setting forth an open plane
(sidereal space as expiation).

And the stellar breeze of a misnamed
phenomenon can be seen well

in a nebula's cast-off shroud.

PALINODE

Strange gods occupied no space in that chaotic inflation of dark
and light,

or in the exponential expansion of a singular disturbance
projecting dark-matter wind

and the seas, cooled to within a fraction of waiting

(*let the dry land appear . . .*)
(*let it divide the waters from the waters*).

Here, a sudden June rain disturbs the weakly interacting leaves
of the hickory, of the birch,

and above me they begin their damp and leathery imprinting
again, on the sky—

on the tarnished outridings inscribed in a mass of starlings
giving wing—

No feeling of gravity: just these starlings veering in swift updrafts
within this hueless radius

(other winds may ease their kind)

Now giving degree and weight to future vacancies, and holding
discourse with nothing but air,

they are such light signatures of sources they do not assume.
I close my eyes, to hear the wind's agitation:

the many implements and the many segments and particulates
these birds stir—

the limbs, boughs, other words here without lack or abundance
(. . . *and watered the whole . . . of the ground*)

in an indeterminate curvature, nearly impossible to follow—

OCEAN DESCANT

I.

And together we're pulled closer into the absence,
permeated by recurrent distortions in our knowledge—

our luminous arguments spun out, our rare velocities radiating
from an emptiness at the core—

And now our ruling differences are all flaws in equivalent flow
(our old iconicity of greening sheaf, of sheet)

All our sweet purchases already starting toward inversion—
All matter draining energy from the gravitational field—

II.

Unraveling wave, stringent fluidity
holding the inversions, the aqueous
version so certain in its dragging:
kelp, crab, conch, whelk, the pebbles
and glass, wooden planks
and a barnacled clatter of gulls . . . .
Graveled alluvion.
All distance hauls.

III.

An imprint in the shape of its own erasure—
pressing itself into pattern, and disparity, in the ashen light—

And the bodies, the limbs and faces, rough with it,
unfinished in their marble enclosures

(sufficient in their own kind of life—)

IV.

Rain opening, apparently indefinite.
Working inside an isotropic, flanking wind,

precipitate downpours tear at the netting
of our contending inventions—

and at all our erratic inveighing—
A leveling, brackish wind shifts

inside our empty lexicon, accumulating
differences, sharpening them—

its cantillation scraping
at the inexorable lovers
(infalling matter)

using us away—
to the underside of wave,
to the salt vicinities.

VIA NEGATIVA

Forbidden to take any *form, shape* or *resemblance* . . .
the way unerringly even now, even breaths in a well-lit

wilderness, bodied in redolent likeness (*frame* and *figure*,
edifice and *structure* . . .). In a supplementary, iterative

laughter, the voices aver in fevered plume—in the waves'
bright spray casting the empty faces—still and still moving.

Such is this synecdochic doubling of lapses in hydraulic
undertow, scanning the excellence and sorting the waters.

Nothing changes; light's traveling, deciphering a chain
to become a body written there, consonant with night

shallows. Sometimes only the sea encloses us for days:
no exceptional tract of dust or bone or wind to convey

love held fast (forming rib, the narrowing stead . . .)
In a manifest world broken by rough claim, flesh—

earth's share—is scored by all those no longer living now.

VII

APOPHATIC

Low-tide shoals flat-lit
and contused.

The night's bittersweet and phosphorous
like a gravitational imprint

(force and matter no different in the end . . .).

Traffic's quarrying its margin—
all arrival and Lethean assemblage—

antiparticles ribbing the ink-wet shallows
(earlier, in daylight, a squall of gulls).

Blacker now, until the mild stars begin
to turn inside the nonluminous matter—

in the governing sea of neutrinos—

§

(Stay awhile in me)
(*All that I ask is that my error last* . . .)

§

In the void
some sacrifice—

some wildness beginning
to thrive—

§

I watch the tide drift into partitions,
mutely in the marshes—

its absorption and dispossession
of the inlet, the stars, the palisade

of cars starting up around me—

§

Then a gale, all edge and factual aftermath
begins over the buoys and wild hibiscus

(replicas in an ocean's slur and graphitic
wreckage—

that immersion in which you were always
lost to me—)

and then over the waters of the earth that will not
remember us.

NOTES

Ere Long: The quoted lines in the fourth stanza are from Zsuzanna Budapest's *The Holy Book of Women's Mysteries* (Wingbow Press, 1989).

A Veil of Multiple Orders is for Quintin James Emerson and Benjamin Dillon Emerson.

As Slightly as the Routes of Stars: The poem's title is taken from Dickinson's poem #993.

The Veil (p. 35) and *Black Veil* were written in response to the veil paintings of Morris Louis and in particular to "Dalet Lamed" (1958) and "Dalet Tet" (1959) respectively. *The Veil* (p. 35) is for Brenda Hillman. *Black Veil* is for Adalaide Morris.

Sea Gate: The poem owes much to Julia Kristeva's work on abjection in *Powers of Horror* (Trans. Leon S. Roudiez, Columbia University Press, 1982); to Judith Butler's work on the materialization of the body as a projected, discursive phenomenon in *Bodies that Matter: On the Discursive Limits of "Sex"* (Routledge, 1993); and to Foucault's *Discipline and Punish: The Birth of the Prison* (Trans. Alan Sheridan, Vintage Books, 1995).

The closing line of the first section is from one of Emily Dickinson's letters to Susan Gilbert Dickinson following the death of Emily's nephew Gilbert Dickinson from typhoid on 5 October 1883: "Moving on in the Dark like Loaded Boats at Night, though there is no Course, there is Boundlessness—" (L 871 in *The Letters of Emily Dickinson*, Ed. Thomas H. Johnson, Harvard University Press, 1965).

In section III, "[R]igid with refuse and the dust of stars" is from Georg Trakl's poem *De Profundis* in *Autumn Sonata* (Trans. Daniel Simko, Moyer Bell, 1989).

On the Apparition of a Substantive: The title of the poem is taken from Emmanuel Levinas' analysis of hypostasis: "Hypostasis . . . is not only the apparition of a new grammatical category; it signifies the suspension of the anonymous *there is*, the apparition of a private domain, of a noun. On the ground of the *there is* a being arises" (*Existence and Existents*, Trans. Alphonso Lingis, The Hague, Martinus Nijhoff, 1978). Seán Hand notes: " 'There is' is anonymous and impersonal being in general, like 'it is raining' . . . . It exists prior even to nothingness . . . It marks the end of objectivizing consciousness, since it is not an object of perception or thought, and cannot be grasped or intentionally constituted. As such, one cannot avoid the experience of the 'there is', since one is steeped in it . . . . Prior to the essence of Being . . . Levinas sees an eternal vigilance which we cannot avoid by falling asleep, and which therefore characterizes existence as bathed in infinity" (*The Levinas Reader*, Ed. Seán Hand, Basil Blackwell, 1989). The dispersed lines "Between both moons,/before dying and after living,/we are a bone of looking/lying beside a sea that never begins" are from Roberto Juarroz's *Second Vertical Poetry* (1963) in *Vertical Poetry* (Trans. W.S. Merwin, North Point Press, 1988).

The Rivers We're Eyeing is after John Clare's poem "Autumn."

Architecture II: The quoted lines in stanza four are from the composer John Tavener's (1944—) 1981 work *Funeral Ikos*, text translated from the Greek by Isabel Hapgood. The poem is in memory of George Carlyle Pittman Jr. (1957-1994), and for L. Mark Slawson.

Imaginary Weather is in memory of David Ellingsworth (1963-1994).

Spring Argument is after Helen Frankenthaler's 1987 painting *Spring Veil*; "adventive" is after Bacon's usage in *The Advancement of Learning* (1605).

Palinode is for Huston Diehl.

Ocean Descant: Section III alludes to Michelangelo's "unfinished" sculptures, and in particular to his last sculpture, the *Rondanini Pietà* (at the Castello Sforzesco in Milan). "Ashen light" (or "earth-shine") was an important early modern cultural term in which artistic, scientific, political and religious debates converged. (It refers to the light of the sun, reflected by the earth, which partially illuminates the dark portion of the moon.) Mentioned by da Vinci in an unpublished notebook of the early 16th century, Johannes Kepler published a full explanation of it in his *Astronomia pars Optica* (1604). It was with the publication of Galileo's *Sidereus Nuncis* (1610) that the phenomenon gained wider scientific currency. Contemporary astronomers at Caltech and elsewhere are currently planning long-term studies of earthshine as an indicator of the earth's climatic changes.

Via Negativa: The poem draws on a number of Protestant iconoclastic tracts, and in particular on Henry Ainsworth's 1624 Protestant polemic *An Arrow Against Idolatrie* in John Calvin's *Institutes of the Christian Religion* (Ed. John T. McNeill, Trans. Ford Lewis Battles, Philadelphia, Westminster Press [c1960]).

Apophatic: "*All that I ask is that my error last*" is a slightly reworded line from Petrarch's canzone 129 (Trans. Mark Musa, Indiana University Press, 1999).

RECENT TITLES FROM ALICE JAMES BOOKS

Alice James Books has been publishing exclusively poetry since 1973. One of the few presses in the country that is run collectively, the cooperative selects manuscripts for publication through both regional and national annual competitions. New authors become active members of the cooperative, participating in the editorial decisions of the press. The press, which places an emphasis on publishing women poets, was named for Alice James, sister of William and Henry, whose fine journal and gift for writing were unrecognized within her lifetime.

Printing by Thomson-Shore
Design and typesetting by Dede Cummings